Funky
PHOBIAS

WRITTEN BY
CORINNE PYLE

ILLUSTRATED BY
DANIEL JANKOWSKI

DESIGNED BY
MICHELLE MARTIN

Special thanks to Dr. Donald Dossey,
author and founder of the
Phobia Institute/Stress Management Centers
of Southern California,
for all his help.

ISBN 0-439-59847-8

1 3 5 7 9 10 8 6 4 2

DO OTTERS MAKE YOU SCREAM IN HORROR?

DO YOU PANIC AT THE SIGHT OF A BRUSSEL SPROUT?

Don't laugh. (There's a fear of laughter, too, by the way.) If you have a phobia, something that seems ordinary to most people can fill you with terror.

A phobia is an extreme fear of an object, activity, or situation. Being afraid of otters or vegetables may not make sense to you, but that's the point. Phobias don't make sense. Let's say you have a phobia of cats, for example. Just seeing a picture of a cat or a toy stuffed cat can cause you to feel intense fear. In your head you know a picture of a cat can't hurt you, but your body still reacts as if it can.

Are you brave enough to face some of the world's strangest fears? Then start reading and find out for yourself what it's like to experience each of these funky phobias.

ALEKTOROPHOBIA

(UH LEHK TORE UH FOH BEE UH)

You've had your dog, Roscoe, since you were two. You've been on a camel ride at the county fair. You've petted goats, scratched the belly of an alligator, and wrapped a snake around your shoulders. Animals are definitely not a problem for you. But get near a chicken and your palms sweat, your heart pounds, your knees weaken, and you feel like you might faint. You're in full-blown panic mode and all you can think is, "Run! Run! Run!" Even pictures of chickens are sometimes enough to leave you trembling. What's wrong with you? You have **alektorophobia**—fear of chickens.

How does a fear of chickens begin? Maybe it started innocently. As a special treat for your third birthday, your parents took you to a petting zoo. There you were, holding out a handful of food when an overly eager chicken pecked your hand—hard! You started wailing and suddenly there was a crazy confusion of clucking and flapping wings all around you. You screamed and cried, terrified, until your dad picked you up and whisked you away.

Just because you're not especially fond of chickens doesn't mean you have **alektorophobia**. People with this phobia go out of their way to avoid places, such as a petting zoo or a farm, where chickens may be lurking. And they're also often terrorized by the thought of coming across a chicken at places where you would never find one, such as at school or at the mall. Nightmares of standing in line waiting to pay for a new CD when suddenly a chicken comes walking up to them may even keep these people from ever entering a mall!

Fear of Chickens

ARACHIBUTYROPHOBIA

(AR UH KUH BUH TIH RUH FOH BEE UH)

You were so late getting ready for school this morning you skipped breakfast. Big mistake. By third period your stomach was making so much noise people in the next classroom could hear it. Somehow you made it to lunch. You rip open your lunch box and gasp in horror. Is it your mom's liver and broccoli casserole? Worse! It's a peanut butter sandwich. Sure, peanut butter is delicious and a good source of protein. But none of that matters to you. You have **arachibutyrophobia**—fear of peanut butter sticking to the roof of the mouth.

Did you ever see a dog eat peanut butter? Everyone laughs as he flaps his tongue in and out of his mouth trying to dislodge the sticky treat. You can just see yourself making those exact same faces and getting the exact same laughs.

You tell yourself you'll face your fear when you get home. You'll get a jar of peanut butter and a glass of milk. What's the worst thing that could happen? This: Just as you stick a big glob of peanut butter in your mouth, your favorite radio station calls. You'll win $1000 if you can tell them the phrase that pays. You have 10 seconds. You try to say, "We rock the tunes." But with the peanut butter glued inside your mouth it comes out, "Me momma moos." You grab for your milk just as your cat knocks it over. It goes crashing to the ground along with your chance at $1000. That sure is a lot of money. Just to be safe, you decide not to face your fear today after all.

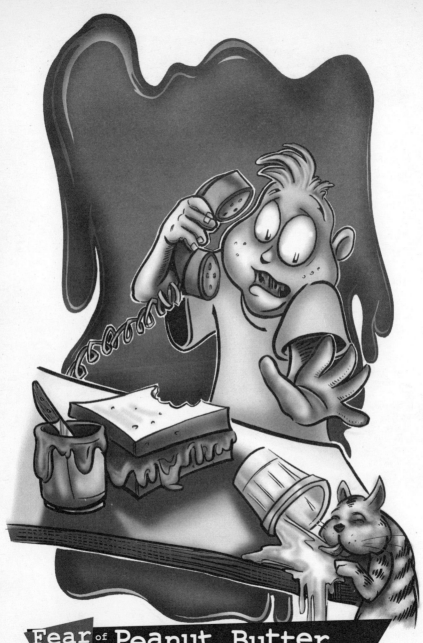

Fear of Peanut Butter Sticking to the Roof of the Mouth

ATAXOPHOBIA

Your brother can really make you mad. Like the time he was returning one of your pencils and made a complete mess in your room. He actually left the pencil on your desk instead of putting it back in its cup. And he sharpened it. You had to sharpen the rest of your pencils so they would all be the same length. Okay, maybe you're more than just neat. You have **ataxophobia**—a fear of disorder or untidiness.

Maybe it became a problem the day Billy Marcus had a piñata at his birthday party. He whacked it with a bat, spilling candy and confetti all over the ground. As you bent to dust off a lollipop, you were tackled by a mob of sugar-crazed party guests. By the time you got up, all the candy was gone. You couldn't find a single piece in the horrible mess of dirt, confetti, and piñata shreds. If you ever have a piñata, you'll carefully cut it open and divide the candy evenly among everyone. It's much more fun (and orderly) that way.

Now your Mom has sent you to camp. She said it would be good for you, but you think she needs a break from you constantly re-organizing the cabinets. So far, camp hasn't been as bad as you thought. The bunks in your cabin are in nice, neat rows. You made yourself a dust pan in arts and crafts. At dinner you say to yourself, "Maybe Mom was right about camp after all." You may have spoken too soon. Just then someone yells out two little words that fill you with panic..."Food fight!" Looks like you better go get that dustpan.

Fear of Disorder or Untidiness

BAROPHOBIA

(BAR UH FOH BEE UH)

You crouch down to get a book out of your bottom row locker.
You carefully dodge Martin Douglas who has the one right above
you. Suddenly, the box of candy bars he is selling for band
falls out of his locker right onto your head. You don't even
notice the pain. All you feel is fear. You have **barophobia**.
No, it's not a fear of candy bars. It's a fear of what made
the candy bars fall—gravity.

It's all Sir Isaac Newton's fault. He discovered gravity
when he saw an apple fall from a tree. You learned that in science
class, where the phobia started. Mrs. Arnold said gravity
keeps everything from floating off the ground. She described it
as an inescapable force constantly pulling on you. It sounded like
something out of a horror movie. Then she told you everything on
earth has gravity. And the more mass it has, the stronger
its pull. All you could think of was trying to break free from
your aunt's huge arms when she hugged you at Thanksgiving.

Some people can avoid the one thing they fear. You can't.
Gravity is everywhere. Or is it? As you head to your
next class you dream you are the world's youngest astronaut.
You imagine floating in gravity-free outer space where
nothing can pull on you or fall on your head. Just then the
bell rings. You come back to Earth to find yourself standing
in the middle of the wrong classroom. Everyone is staring.
One kid laughs so hard that his chair tips over backward and,
just like the tumbing candy bars,
he falls to the ground.
Sometimes gravity
isn't so bad after all.

Fear of Gravity

BOGEYPHOBIA

(BOO GEE FOH BEE UH)

When you were little, this was your bogeyman defense system:

1) Keep your closet door closed. (If the bogeyman was in your closet, you believed the closed door would keep him in there.)

2) Jam lots of junk underneath your bed. (Not only was this a quick way to clean your room, it kept the bogeyman from fitting under there.)

3) Leave a nightlight on. (The bogeyman hates them.)

As long as you followed all three steps, you could handle your **bogeyphobia**—fear of the bogeyman.

One time you woke up in the middle of the night knowing something was wrong. Your nightlight was off. When your eyes adjusted to the dark, you realized that your closet door was open, too. Now you were scared. Maybe a closed closet door couldn't stop the bogeyman after all. Maybe your whole bogeyman defense system didn't work. You spent the rest of the night lying awake in the exact center of your bed, hoping the bogeyman's arms couldn't reach you if he was hiding underneath. Finally, morning came. You raced downstairs and breathlessly told your mom what happened. "What's the matter?" your older brother sneered. "Were you scared the bogeyman was going to get you?" That next night, you couldn't sleep. You kept waiting for the bogeyman to return. After awhile a door creaked open. It was your bedroom door, not the closet. You closed your eyes and peeked to see what was happening. It was your brother. Thinking you were asleep, he snuck over and turned off your nightlight. As he crept over to your closet door to open it a crack, you barked, "It was you!" He let out a startled scream and tripped over himself while trying to escape. "What's the matter?" you asked calmly. "Were you scared the bogeyman was going to get you?"

Fear of the BOGEYMAN

CHIONOPHOBIA

(KIY UH NO FOH BEE UH)

The Eskimos have 20 different words for snow. You have a few yourself, like "pneumonia-giver" and "avalanche-waiting-to happen." You have **chionophobia**—fear of snow.

It starts the same way every year. Against the gray sky you see a tiny, frosty menace drifting towards your town. Your blood turns as cold as the air outside. You know millions more will soon follow. They'll block roads, shut down traffic, and send people running to their homes. There's nothing you can do. The snowflake invasion has begun.

Ever since this year's first flake, the snow's been out to get you. Walking to school this morning, you sank up to your eyeballs in what used to be your front lawn. As you waited for someone to dig you out, you kept calm by counting the days till spring. Now school's over and you're ready to head back home. This time things are going to be different. You make it down the first road and turn a corner, just missing getting sprayed by a passing snowplow. Now you're on your street, but it's completely blocked by a massive snowball fight. Deflecting blow after blow with your science book, you run through without getting hit. Only a few more yards to go. Walking up your driveway, a wall of snow built up by weeks of shoveling starts to collapse. You leap forward, slip on an icy patch, but regain your balance just as the wall collapses behind you. You carefully walk the last few steps to your door and throw your fist in the air. "I did it!" you yell, but just a little too loudly. The noise sends the pile of snow perched on your roof plopping down on your head. Let's see. How many days are there till spring again?

Fear of Snow

COULROPHOBIA

(KAWL RUH FOH BEE UH)

You and your friend are building a go-cart in his basement. He runs upstairs to get some drinks. Suddenly, you get that creepy feeling that something is behind you. You turn around and there it is. You stare into its ghostly white face with the huge red mouth. You feel its eyes follow you as you run up the stairs. You tell your friend you have to go home, but you really just want to get away from that horrible painting. You have **coulrophobia**—fear of clowns.

You wish your parents hadn't taken you to the circus when you were little. Everything was fine until they put you in line to meet the clown. The other kids were excited. You weren't so sure. The closer you got to Cranky the Clown, the bigger he seemed to be. Then your parents shoved you toward him. He stepped forward and his huge foot landed on top of yours. You couldn't get away. You looked to your family for help, but they just laughed. They thought that joker was funny. Finally, he moved and you escaped, but you never looked at clowns the same way again.

Relax, you're not the only one with this phobia. Clowns freak out a lot of people. What is it about them, anyway? Is it the make-up they wear? Are they trying to hide something? Is it their clothes? Everything is either way too big or way too small, and none of it matches. Whatever it is about clowns, you'll just keep your distance for now. And if your family goes to that fast food restaurant where you have to shout your order into the clown's mouth, you'll just stay home.

CYCLOPHOBIA

(SIY KLUH FOH BEE UH)

You see a row of two-wheelers chained to a bike rack.
You know they're locked up because someone might take
them, not because they might get loose and terrorize the
neighborhood. You still cross the street, just in case.
You have **cyclophobia**—fear of bicycles.

The day you learned to ride a bike, your mom put you in
more protective gear than a hockey goalie. Somehow you managed
to climb up onto the seat. Your dad held on as you started to
peddle. "You're doing great," he encouraged. As you looked
back and saw that he had already let go, you realized he
hadn't taught you how to stop. The bike jerked and lurched
from side to side, and then threw you off like a rodeo bull
rider. Somehow the metal monster kept going. It turned and
headed back toward you. Wrapped in so many layers of padding,
you couldn't move. You just lay there helplessly as you got
run over by your own bike.

You'd like to go riding with your friends. You imagine yourself
speeding down a hill, almost flying. Then you imagine the
bike chain grabbing your pant leg. Struggling to get free,
you don't see the pile of dirt coming up ahead of you.
Speeding over it, you soar off the ground. "You got major
air!" your friends yell. You flail your arms, accidentally
knocking the handlebars completely around. "You just did a
bar spin!" they scream. Then you fly over the handlebars,
ripping your pants, and landing with a thud. That's when
your friends would figure out you're not really a BMX
superstar. For you, just getting near
a bike is an extreme sport.

Fear of Bicycles

EiSOPTROPHOBiA

(iCE OP TROH FOH BEE UH)

To read the following riddle, hold it up to a mirror:

What turns everything around but always tells the truth? Answer: A mirror

If you couldn't force yourself to read this riddle, you have **eisoptrophobia**—fear of mirrors.

A lot of **eisoptrophobia** is based on old superstitions about mirrors. People once believed that if something happened to your reflection, it happened to you, too. Seeing a broken or distorted image of yourself was considered a very bad omen. The superstition that breaking a mirror brings bad luck is still around today. Basutos, a group of people in South Africa, believe that crocodiles can get you just by snapping at your reflection in the water. This may not be true, but if a crocodile is close enough to snap at your reflection, that's definitely a bad omen anyway.

You're playing Truth or Dare at Lisa Zelver's slumber party. You pick "dare." Lisa decides you have to look into the bedroom mirror and say, "Mirror, mirror on the wall, show us something to surprise us all." You know this dare would only work for the evil queen in Snow White, but you still don't want to do it. You and two of your friends stand looking in the mirror. You close your eyes, take a deep breath, and cautiously say, "Mirror, mirror... on the wall... show us something to surprise us all." Slowly you open your eyes. All you see in the mirror are yourself and your two friends. Just as you start to relax, a fourth face appears. You scream. Then everyone screams, including the mysterious face that just appeared. Wait a minute—that's Lisa's mom. She just walked up behind you to see how things were going. Truth or Dare ends and everyone starts giving each other makeovers. You don't bother to check your new look in the mirror. You're sure it's just fine.

EREUTHOPHOBIA

(ER oo THOH FOH BEE UH)

Your school is having a special assembly tonight. They're going to announce the winner of the annual essay contest. Since you're one of the finalists, your dad made you go. You say you really don't care if you win or not, but that's just a lie. You're secretly hoping you'll lose. Then you won't have to get up in front of everyone, and they won't see your face turn redder than the exit sign you're thinking about running toward. You have **ereuthophobia**—fear of blushing.

The fear of blushing is a social phobia. (The fear of being stared at, which you'll read about later, is another.) People with social phobias are afraid of being embarrassed or made fun of in public. Your **ereuthophobia** makes you worry about blushing the second any attention is focused on you. Of course, worrying about it just makes you blush more. Maybe this is one of those fears you'll eventually outgrow. For some reason, people blush most often during adolescence. Things could get better if you can just make it through the next few years. Right now you just want to make it through this assembly.

They finally announce the winner of the essay contest. It's you. Everyone is smiling and clapping as you cross the stage. Hey, this isn't so bad after all. In fact, it's kind of nice. Then you see your dad running down the aisle. He's kind of hard to miss. He's wearing a tee shirt with your picture on it and yelling, "That's my baby." With one hand he's waving wildly. With the other hand he's zooming in on you with his video camera, capturing your quickly changing facial color for all time. You may have just figured out why people blush so much during adolescence. A lot of kids must have parents just as embarrassing as yours.

Fear of Blushing

FELINOPHOBIA

(FEE LINE UH FOH BEE UH)

Cats are the most popular pets in the United States. All over the country, sane people take them into their homes and feed them, care for them, and even clean out their litter boxes. But as far as you're concerned, it's all part of a feline plan to take over the planet. You have **felinophobia**—fear of cats.

Felinophobia is one of the most common animal fears. It could be the way a cat's eyes glow in the dark that makes this fear so common. It could be the way they dart back and forth in front of your feet when you're trying to walk down the stairs. For whatever reason, **felinophobia** has been around for a long time. In the Middle Ages people in England thought witches could turn into black cats. This made cats pretty unpopular for awhile. Soon there were fewer and fewer cats around England. That's when more and more mice started showing up. Eventually the people decided cats weren't so bad after all. After that, only mice in England suffered from a fear of cats.

Cats can make over 100 vocal sounds, each with a different meaning. One meow might mean, "Hello." Another might mean, "I don't like this." (This one is often heard while they are getting a bath.) None of a cat's vocal sounds, however, has been found to mean, "Soon we will take over your planet." Who knows? Maybe cats do want to take over the Earth. And maybe they could even do it. But this is an animal that sleeps 16 hours a day, and is still sleepy after that. It's pretty hard to take over an entire planet between naps.

Fear of Cats

GELIOPHOBIA

(JEEL EE UH FOH BEE UH)

You dread third period. The class clown sits right next to you.
You try not to look at him, but you can't help it. He's making
a frog face by pulling back the sides of his face and sticking
out his tongue. You snicker and quickly try to cover it with a
cough. Mr. Brown gives you a warning glare, then continues with
his lesson. The class clown goes back to making faces, but now
he's moving his mouth to match what the teacher is saying. All of
your muscles tense. You're sweating and your eyes are watering.
The harder you try to hold it back, the more the laughter
builds inside. Finally, it erupts. Mr. Brown gives you both
detention for having "too much fun during class." But you're
not having fun. Being trapped next to Frog Face is more like
torture. You have **geliophobia**—fear of laughter.

Laughter relieves stress for most people, but not for
you. You're afraid if you let loose a little bit, something
bad will happen. People are always telling you that you're
too serious. They try to loosen you up by telling you jokes
or even tickling you. They just don't understand. **Geliophobia**
is nothing to laugh at.

You report to Mr. Brown's classroom after school and sit as far
from the class clown as possible. The teacher says, "I'm sure
you can both sit quietly without any silliness. If not, you'll
have detention every day until you can." The joker nods, but as
soon as Mr. Brown turns away he looks at you with his eyelids
flipped inside out. You struggle with all your might to hold the
laugh in, but you know it's going to burst out. At this rate,
you may have detention for the rest of your life.

Fear of Laughter

HiPPOPOTOMONSTROS-
ESQUiPPEDALiOPHOBiA

(HiP UH PAH TAH MAHN STROH SES-
KWUH PUH DAYL EE OH FOH BEE UH)

It's the third round of your school's spelling bee. You wince
as the teacher says, "Spell metamorphosis." Sweat collects
on your forehead. Your heartbeat pounds in your ears, and the
room starts to spin. "I can't take it anymore!" you yell as
you run out of the auditorium. The pressure was just too much.
It would have been even worse if you had actually been in the
contest and not just sitting in the audience. You have...oh,
boy...you're not going to like this...
hippopotomonstrosesquippedaliophobia—fear of long words.

To people with this phobia, the name must seem like a cruel
joke. It might help if we broke it down into parts. First we
have **hippopoto-** as in "big as a hippo." Then comes **-monstro-**
as in "monstrous", which means "really big." Now all we have
left is **-sesquipeddaliophobia.** Okay, **-ped-** means "foot," **-
sesqui-** means "and a half," and **-aliophobia** means "relating to
the fear of something." So we're talking about a fear of words
that are a foot and a half long. Wow. The person who named this
phobia must have really wanted people to face their fear.

Some people say the best way to tackle a phobia is in steps.
Let's say you're afraid of words over 10 letters long.
First, face 11-letter words until you get comfortable with
them. There, you just faced one. Comfortable is 11 letters long.
Now that you've accomplished that, try a 12-letter word.
Hey, accomplished is a 12-letter word. Congratulations.
Wait. That has 15 letters. See, you're doing great. Pretty soon
you'll be able to hear the name of your phobia without feeling
dizzy. Spelling it, though...that's a whole different story.

Hippopotomonstrosesquippedaliopho

Fear of Long Words

HOMICHLOPHOBIA

(HOH MIHK LOH FOH BEE UH)

Yesterday you saw the fog waiting on a hill. Soon it would creep down and make your whole town look like those spooky old movies where a creepy castle is wrapped in a cold, gray cloud, and you never know what's hiding in the mist. You hate those movies. You have **homichlophobia**—fear of fog.

When you woke up this morning, the fog had already arrived. Waiting at the school bus stop, you're completely surrounded by it. Things you see everyday suddenly seem strange and different. That shape on the corner could be a big dog ready to pounce. When you turn your flashlight on it, it's only a shrub. Putting the flashlight away, you hear footsteps. Who could that be? You're the only person who waits at this bus stop. Now your **homichlophobia** is completely taking over. You decide to head back home and ask for a ride to school. To avoid whoever or whatever it is heading in your direction, you take the long way around the block and head for home. You're almost there when you hear the footsteps again. Whatever it is must be following you. You aim your flashlight at a spot in the fog, but the battery is dead. You freeze. The footsteps are getting closer and closer. Remembering all those scary movies, you fling the flashlight toward the sound and run the rest of the way home.

You get inside your house and slam the door. "Are you looking for the book report you forgot?" Your mom asks. "Your dad went out in this fog to bring it to you at the bus stop. Did you see him?" "Uh...nope," you answer honestly. "I must have missed him." At least you hope you did when you flung that flashlight.

Fear of Fog

HYLOPHOBIA

(HI LEH FOH BEE UH)

When you were little, your babysitter told you stories to help you sleep. One night she read you *Hansel and Gretel* and *Little Red Riding Hood*. These children went into the woods and almost ended up as dinner for a witch and a wolf, giving the term "kids meal" a whole new meaning. The stories didn't make you sleepy. In fact, you were awake for days. Your babysitter didn't know you had **hylophobia**—fear of forests.

Hansel and Gretel and *Little Red Riding Hood* are both Grimm's fairy tales. The brothers Grimm collected these stories about 200 years ago, and they've been causing **hylophobia** ever since. A lot of the stories are about terrible things happening to kids in the forest. But you're a lot smarter than Little Red Riding Hood. She couldn't tell the difference between her grandma and a wolf in a nightgown. If Little Red made it out of the woods okay, so can you.

Clutching your *Wilderness Survival* book, you've agreed to go on a family camping trip. The book says you should never go anywhere in the forest alone, which is just fine with you. So you force your sister to walk with you to the restroom, and wait outside. Of course when you're ready to head back, she's gone. Taking a tip from your survival book and Hansel and Gretel, you marked a trail so you could find your way back. But wait. The markers are gone, too. After a panic attack and a quick check of your book, you blow the emergency signal on your whistle. Just then your sister appears. She was on the other side of the building the entire time. You didn't see her or the trail you marked because you walked out the wrong door of the restroom. Wouldn't you know it? That's the one situation your *Wilderness Survival* book missed.

Fear of Forests

ichthyophobia

You're drifting on a boat on a lake. You're so relaxed you fall asleep. Then something touches your hand, which is dangling in the water. Suddenly you're wide-awake. You try to jump to your feet but end up falling out of the boat and into the lake. Now you feel them surrounding you, ready to touch you with their puckering lips at any second. You jolt out of the water and back into the boat practically before you can get wet. You have **ichthyophobia**—fear of fish.

You actually owned a fish once. You won it at a carnival. It seemed harmless enough until you had to clean its water. You went to scoop out the little gold critter in a net, but it wiggled out and landed on the floor. You had to grab it while it flopped all over the kitchen floor. Feeling its cold, slimy, body squirming in your bare hands was the beginning of your **ichthyophobia**. After that, you never wanted to change that poor fish's water again. Eventually, the bowl turned green with algae. Then it got even uglier. You couldn't see the fish anymore, just the water moving where it swam.

On the first day of school, you were all dressed in green with your hair hanging past your shoulders. You thought you looked pretty good until your grandma said, "Oh, you look just like a mermaid!" She meant it as a compliment, but it was the wrong thing to say. Your poor grandma never knew why you ran back into your room and changed your clothes. There was no way you were going to the first day of school looking like a fish.

Fear of Fish

KERAUNOPHOBIA

(KEH RAW NO FOH BEE UH)

FLASH_1-2-3-4-5-6-7-8-9-10-11-12_BooM!

You always count the seconds between the lightning and the thunder to see how far away they are. Every five seconds equals one mile between you and them. This clever little trick helped you when you used to have **keraunophobia**—fear of thunder and lightning.

FLASH_1-2-3-4-5-6-7-8-9_BooM!

It's getting closer. Your dog Hank just crept by on his belly. He still has **keraunophobia**. "Remember when I used to be afraid and Dad told me that story about the thunder and lightning?" you ask Hank, who is now cowering in your closet. "He told me Native Americans believed they were made when the thunderbird flew across the sky. It was enormous, with feathers as big as canoes. When it flapped its wings, it caused the thunder. When it opened and closed its glowing eyes, it caused the lightning. That story didn't help much, did it, Hank? I still..."

FLASH_1-2-3-4-5_KA BooM!

It's only a mile away. You're shaking now. It must be because you're cold. "When I used to get scared, I would play music really loud LIKE THIS," you tell Hank as you crank up the volume on your CD player. "THEN I COULDN'T HEAR MYSELF THINK. SEE, I'M DEFINITELY NOT THINKING ABOUT THE THUNDER AND LIGHTNING CLOSING IN ON US RIGHT NOW. AND I'M NOT PICTURING THAT HUGE BIRD WITH THE CANOE FEATHERS AND LASER EYES HEADING TOWARD THE HOUSE. I'M JUST..."

FLASH_1-2_CRRR-ACK!!!

"IT'S HERE!" Good thing you got over your **keraunophobia**, or you'd be really scared. Isn't that nice? Hank does look awfully nervous there in that closet. I'm sure he appreciates you climbing in there with him, just to keep him company.

Fear of Thunder and Lightning

LACHANOPHOBIA

(LUH KAWN UH FOH BEE UH)

You tried to slip them into your napkin, but your mom caught you. You hid some under your mashed potatoes, but she saw that too. There's got to be some way to get out of eating your vegetables. Just then your dog comes running into the kitchen. Perfect. You hold a broccoli stalk out to him under the table. He runs up and sniffs it, then keeps going. Great. Can dogs have **lachanophobia**—fear of vegetables?

All your life your mom's told you veggies are good for you, and they'll make you strong. You know they're full of important minerals, but so are rocks. You'd almost rather eat a few of them than the cold, mushy broccoli bunches lying there on your plate.

"Have you ever heard of **lachanophobia**?" you ask your mom. "It's the fear of vegetables, and it's for real." You've gotten her attention. "Making a kid with **lachanophobia** eat vegetables is like sticking a kid who's afraid of lightning out in a storm." It's working. She's actually feeling guilty for wanting you to eat them. "Alright, forget about the veggies tonight," she says. "Go do your homework." "The thing is," you add hopefully, "I have a fear of homework, too." You should have quit while you were ahead. **Lachanophobia** is a real phobia, but you don't really have it. What you have is a *strong dislike* for veggies. "Nice try," your mom says, leaving the room. "Just eat one bite, okay?" You rush to the window, hoping to fling the veggies out before she comes back. It's stuck. The thought of eating the broccoli makes you gather up all your strength and pull open the window with a mighty yank. "Mom was right," you think as you fling a handful out onto your side yard. "Vegetables really do make you strong."

Fear of Vegetables

LUTRAPHOBIA

(LEW TRUH FOH BEE UH)

Your family was spending the day at the beach. Everyone was in the water but you. Remembering your mom's rule, you kept eating every half-hour so she wouldn't let you swim. You just felt safer on dry land. You knew *they* were out there somewhere, waiting... watching...frolicking. You have **lutraphobia**—fear of otters.

A lot of people think otters are cute. That's what they want you to think. It may look like they're always smiling, but you know that expression is really a vicious sneer. You're not taken in by those soft, round eyes either. Those are the same eyes that they creepily keep open underwater as they stalk their prey. And what about those great big brown noses? All the better to smell you with, my dear.

You're happy your science teacher is showing a video today... until you find out it's about otters. Sitting in the darkened classroom, you can barely watch the terrifying sight as an otter slides down a muddy bank. Well, actually that was kind of cute. Oh, but now things are really going to get scary. There's an otter wrapping itself in seaweed so it won't float away while it sleeps. See, now that's really...well, that's pretty cute, too. You start to think, "Maybe these little guys aren't so bad. Maybe next time I'm at the beach, I can actually go in the water." Now the video is showing an otter floating happily on its back. "Oh, how sweet," you think. "The little rascal has a rock on its belly and it's pounding a clam on it. It's pounding it over and over again. Now it's got the clam open and it's ripping apart the meat with its long... sharp...pointy...teeth." Oh, well. Looks like you'll be doing all your swimming in swimming pools for awhile longer.

Fear of Otters

MELOPHOBIA

You're trapped in the backseat on a road trip with your family. Your dad has been playing his "Greatest Hits of the 70s" collection on the CD player since he pulled out of the driveway. It's a 10-volume set he ordered from a late-night TV infomercial. For the foreseeable future you are going to hear every disco tune ever recorded. And as far as you can tell, your family is going to sing along with every single one. Your palms are sweaty, your mouth is dry, and there's a strange thump, thump, thumping in your chest. Oh no, your heart is already pounding to a disco beat and you haven't even made it through Volume 1! You have **melophobia**—fear of music.

Most people with **melophobia** are only afraid of one type of music, like disco for example. Other people are afraid of a musical instrument. The composer Wolfgang Amadeus Mozart was terrified of trumpets as a boy. To help him get over it, his dad asked the court trumpet player to blast him with his horn. Didn't work. Poor Wolfie was still afraid of the trumpet, and probably the trumpet player, too.

New types of music have always scared people. Thousands of years ago the philosopher Plato said musical change "is full of danger to the whole State and ought to be prohibited." In the Middle Ages, some musical scales were outlawed because they thought the notes had a bad effect on people. Today a lot of parents think some rock and rap music is dangerous. And someday your kids might listen to music that you'll think is a little scary. Will it be heavy metal played on nose rings? Nails being scraped across chalkboards? Worse yet, maybe disco will make a comeback.

METEOROPHOBIA

(MEE TEE AWR UH FOH BEE UH)

You and a friend are sitting on her front porch one night.
Looking up she sees a meteor flash across the sky.
"Hey, it's a shooting star," she says, calling the meteor
by its popular nickname. "Let's make a wish." You would,
but you suddenly remember you have to run home and hide under
your bed. You have **meteorophobia**—fear of meteors.

Just what are meteors? They're tiny space rocks that make
a streak of light when they plunge through our atmosphere—
hurtling toward Earth. If any part of the rock makes it to
Earth without burning up, it's called a meteorite.
They're the things you really worry about. Especially since
you heard the theory that a huge meteorite wiped out
the dinosaurs. Now, you know most meteorites are tiny,
and the odds of getting hit by something falling from space
are trillions to one. But still, tell that to the dinosaurs.

Superman's home planet, Krypton, exploded right after he left
for Earth. Pieces of it, called Kryptonite, rained down as
meteorites. Now if he ever gets near a piece, the Man
of Steel turns into a pile of jelly. All the superhero stuff
disappears and he's just another guy in tights and a cape. He may
run faster than a speeding bullet and bend steel with his bare
hands, but even Superman is afraid of some meteorites.
So the next time someone says, "Look! Up in the sky!" go ahead.
If you don't, you might miss a bird, a plane, or a superhero
who's scared of things just like the rest of us. If it is a
meteor, you can always move faster than a speeding bullet
back under your bed.

Fear of Meteors

METROPHOBIA

(MEH TRUH FOH BEE UH)

Rhyming verses scare you,
  you can't disagree.
You have **metrophobia**—
  the fear of...the stuff written by poets.

Humpty Dumpty is the rhyme
  that started it all.
You got scared when poor Humpty
  had a big...tumble.

Now when music is playing
  you don't sing along.
Lyrics are really just poems
  that are part of a...tune.

You'd completely freeze up
  if you ever had to rap.
The crowd would be silent.
  Nobody would...applaud.

And why don't poets say what they mean
  when they're writing an ode?
Poems are hard to decipher,
  like they're in a secret...language.

We came close to rhyming,
  as close as we could.
But we wouldn't do that to you.
  Well, maybe we would.

44

Fear of POETRY

MYTHOPHOBIA

(MiHTH UH FOH BEE UH)

You've heard how George Washington chopped down his father's cherry tree when he was a boy. When his father asked him if he knew what had happened to the tree, little George said, "I can't tell a lie. I did cut it with my hatchet." You can relate to this, not because you're a tree whacker, but because you have **mythophobia**—fear of lying.

You're terrified of lying. You know that sooner or later you'll get caught. Let's just say you were in George's buckle shoes. Your first instinct would be to say, "What cherry tree? I don't know anything about a cherry tree." But every time you passed by the stump where the tree used to be, you'd just know the guilty look on your face would give you away. You'd keep waiting for your dad to notice the tree sap on your hatchet or wood chips on your shoes. You'd drive yourself crazy wondering if your sister or brother secretly saw the whole thing and was just waiting for the perfect moment to turn you in. When your dad asked you about the tree, you'd do exactly what George did. Better to confess and get it over with. Any punishment your dad would give you couldn't compare to what you'd put yourself through.

We've all learned this story about George Washington and its lesson about the importance of telling the truth. The funny thing is, though, it never really happened. It's just a myth written by a man named Mason Locke Weems. Unlike you, he didn't have **mythophobia**. Weems basically told a lie to explain Washington's honesty. Hmmm. Wonder what old George would think about that?

Fear of Lying

MYXOPHOBIA

(MIK SO FOH BEE UH)

Your mom told you all week to take out the trash. Now you wake to hear the garbage truck heading down the street. All you can think about is how much trouble you'll be in if that garbage isn't out on the curb when the truck gets to your house. You grab the bag and head outside. Taking a step, barefoot in your PJs, you feel something wiggly and slippery move under your foot. Full panic hits as you realize you are standing on a slug. You jump and fling the bag into the air, sending a week's worth of slick, squishy grossness all over the yard. Rotten banana peels, egg shells with runny white film inside and, worst of all, thousands of used tissues from your sister's nasty nose surround you. You dodge and weave through the slimefield and disappear inside the house just as the garbage truck rolls past. Now you remember why you put off taking out the garbage for so long. You have **myxophobia**—fear of slime.

Some people are afraid of slimy foods like oysters or the meatloaf in your school cafeteria (well, everyone is afraid of that). Others panic around slimy animals, or animals that just look slimy. They've heard that snakes are really dry and scaly, but they still won't go near one. To someone with **myxophobia**, looking slimy can be just as bad as being slimy.

Actually, a lot of kids like slime. They buy it at toy stores. They go on game shows and have it poured on their heads. Who knows? Maybe the next time you're on garbage duty, one of those kids will take the trash out for you.

Fear of Slime

OPHTHALMOPHOBIA

(OFF THAL MO FOH BEE UH)

You're supposed to be giving an oral book report, but you can't even remember the book's name. The longer you stand there, the more your class stares. They are all waiting for you to say something. You're waiting for the same thing. In order to talk you have to breathe, and that's not happening at the moment. You have **ophthalmophobia**—fear of being stared at.

Ophthalmophobia ruined a lot of breakfasts when you were younger. Before your older brother even came into the kitchen, you knew he was somewhere in the house, staring at you. As soon as he walked into the room you yelled, "Stop staring at me!" "Why would I want to stare at you?" he asked, pretending to ignore you as he ate his cereal. He kept his eyes on his bowl the entire time, but you weren't fooled for a second. "Mom, he's staring at me!" you yelled. Since this had become the routine at your breakfast table for the past three years, she no longer seemed to hear you. You were forced, once again, to build a wall of cereal boxes between you and your brother. You ate your breakfast, but you didn't enjoy it. Somewhere behind the box of Silly O's you knew you were being stared at.

It's easy to get nervous when people are looking at you. You're sure you'll embarrass yourself by tripping or having something hanging out of your nose. It might seem safer to stay in the background, but that can keep you from meeting new people or doing your best in school. So go ahead, risk a little embarrassment. But keep a tissue handy—just in case.

POGONOPHOBIA

(POH GUH NAH FOH BEE UH)

You have a toy called "Fuzzy Freddy." At first Freddy isn't fuzzy at all. He's completely bald. You take a magnet and move metal shavings around his head and face to give him hair. Thanks to you, Freddy is now sporting a lovely beehive hairdo and a giant unibrow above his eyes. You add ear hair flowing past his shoulders to complete his new look. Just as you finish his makeover, a speck of metal hair accidentally lands right under his lower lip. Suddenly, Freddy is just too freaky. You fling him across the room and decide Freddy is fine without fuzz. As far as you're concerned, bald is beautiful - especially when it comes to chins. You have **pogonophobia**—fear of beards.

It's hard to say where a fear of beards comes from. Some people see beards as a disguise. They think a bearded person (or toy, in the case of Freddy) must have something to hide. Sure, Santa Claus seems nice, but how well do we really know him? Other times it's not what the beard is hiding, but what's hiding inside the beard. Some whiskers are so bushy most of the person's breakfast and maybe even his car keys could be hanging out in there.

If you have **pogonophobia**, try to remember that it's not always easy being fuzzy faced. Peter the Great once put a tax on beards. Today being whiskerless still has its advantages. When clean-cut men run for office, they usually get 5% more votes than a bearded opponent does. So before you scream in horror, remember that life can be tough on men with beards—and even tougher on women who have them.

Fear of Beards

PHOBIA

Your aunt is into marionettes big time. She even has a little theater set up for them. You'll never forget the first—and last—show she ever put on for you. You were a little kid sitting alone in front of the stage. She was hidden above it, pulling the puppet's strings. The puppet danced and danced around until suddenly it just froze. You sat for what seemed like forever watching it hang there, motionless. You called out to your aunt, but she didn't answer. Finally, you slowly crept up to the stage. Looking into the puppet's unblinking eyes, you reached out to touch it. Just then your aunt made the puppet spring back to life, causing you to jump back at least three rows. You hope your aunt didn't mind your running off before the show was over. You have **pupaphobia**—fear of puppets.

It's not just marionettes. Hand puppets are scary, too. You saw a puppet show once where a crocodile kept popping up behind some puppet that looked like a clown. The kids tried to warn the clown but he wouldn't listen. Finally, he got bitten on his hooked nose before fighting off the crocodile with a stick. Your parents think TV shows are too violent. They should check out a puppet show sometime.

Your aunt still doesn't understand that you don't love marionettes as much as she does (but then, does anybody?). She sent you one for your last birthday. The first thing you did was cut off all of its strings so no one could start pulling on them, making the puppet dance around. You know your aunt meant well, but what was she thinking? Everyone knows that when you give someone a gift, there should be no strings attached.

Fear of Puppets

SCOLIONOPHOBIA

(SKOH LEE ON UH FOH BEE UH)

Your alarm clock went off 10 minutes ago and you're still in bed. After calling you five times, your mom comes in to check on you. You tell her your stomach is upset, your head hurts, and you're shaky all over. The trouble is, you tell her the same thing every school day. It's not that you're faking. The thought of school really does make you feel sick. You have **scolionophobia**—fear of school.

Different people have different types of **scolionophobia**. For some people, fear of school is really a fear of leaving home. For others it's a fear of the unknown. For example, going to a new school can trigger this phobia in some kids. Sometimes it's a specific thing about school that causes the fear. Taking a test, speaking in front of the class, trying to fit in with your classmates, even avoiding getting beaned with a dodge ball during PE class can all be scary. If you have **scolionophobia**, the one thing about school that scares you can get bigger and bigger in your mind until you're scared of school itself.

Staying home from school isn't the answer. Sure, it seems like the perfect solution. Your head and stomach would probably feel better the minute your mom said you could miss a day. But skipping school only makes the phobia worse. Besides, you'll just have to make up any classes you miss. So the next time you need help forcing yourself out of bed in the morning, just think of these two words...summer school. Arrrgh! Now that's really scary.

Fear of School

TELEPHONOPHOBIA

(TEH LUH FOH NUH FOH BEE UH)

Alexander Graham Bell was about to test his new invention, the
telephone. His assistant, Thomas A. Watson, was waiting
in another room. Suddenly Bell spilled battery acid on his
clothes and said, "Watson, come here. I want you." Watson heard
the message over the new machine and came to help. The first
telephone call was an emergency situation. Now, thanks
to Bell, for you every call is an emergency situation. You have
telephonophobia—fear of telephones.

All phone calls make you freeze up, especially prank calls.
Your friends talked you into calling your neighbor, mean Mr.
Anderson, once. "Is your refrigerator plugged in?" you asked
him. "Yes." "Then you'd better catch it," you said. You were
so nervous, you got the joke wrong. "Oh, I meant 'Is your
refrigerator running?'" you explained. Your friends were laughing.
Mr. Anderson wasn't. "Who is this?" he growled. You got so
flustered you told him your name and added, "I live next door."
All your friends flew out the back as the pounding started on
the front door. Your **telephonophobia** just got worse after that.

Today you have to call Susan Marshall to get the math homework
assignment. You dial her number, but hang up the phone as
soon as it rings. You'll just practice first. "Hello. Hi. Hi
there. I sit behind you in math. Do you have today's assignment?"
you rehearse. "Okay, here goes. I just hope her brother doesn't
answer." You pick up the phone again and hear someone
laughing on the other end. It's her brother. You didn't hang
up all the way, and he heard everything you said. Forget about
homework. Now fighting off a panic attack is your biggest
problem. You hope you start breathing again soon. You really
don't want to call 9-1-1.

Fear of Telephones

TRISKAIDEKAPHOBIA

(TRIS KIY DECK UH FOH BEE UH)

The name of this phobia comes from the Greek words meaning
"3 and 10 fear." You completely understand why it
was named that way. You would much rather say "3 and
10" than the number they add up to. You have
triskaidekaphobia—fear of the number 13.

There are examples of **triskaidekaphobia** everywhere. Many tall
buildings don't have a 13th floor. When they number the floors,
they skip right from 12 to 14. Some people won't go to any party
if there will be 13 people there. In fact, in France there are
people you can hire to be the 14th guest at a get-together.
(How's that for a great job—being paid to go to parties?)
And, of course, there is Friday the 13th. This is such a
common fear that it has its very own phobia. It's called
paraskavedekatriaphobia. In case you were wondering, every year
has at least one Friday the 13th.

On April 12, 1970, NASA sent a mission to the moon named
Apollo 13. If its name wasn't bad enough, it took off at 1:13pm
(13 minutes past the 13th hour of the day). The next day,
April 13, there was a huge explosion on board that badly
damaged the spacecraft. Many **triskaidekaphobics** point to this
as proof that the number 13 is unlucky, but it all depends on
how you look at it. Even though it seemed hopeless, the astronauts
and the crew at mission control somehow managed to bring the ship
back home safely. In this case, you might even say the number
13 turned out to be pretty lucky.

Fear of the **Number 13**

If you're scared of all the things mentioned in this book, from chickens to the number 13, you probably have **panophobia**—fear of everything. That would mean you're afraid of this book, too. Congratulations on getting all the way through it.

If you aren't scared of any of the things mentioned in this book, your strange fear must have gotten past us, at least for now. Have we come to the end of this batch of funky phobias already? Yes, we're afraid we have.